ARCTIC
EXPEDITION

Library of Congress Cataloging-in-Publication Data
Salisbury, Mike.
        Arctic expedition.

        (Young explorers)
        Summary: Explores how humans and animals live in the harsh conditions of the
Arctic regions.
        1. Arctic regions--Juvenile literature. [1. Arctic regions] I. Johnson, Paul, 1951-   ill.
II. Title. III. Series: Young explorers (Milwaukee, Wis.)
G614.S24   1989   919.8'04   88-42905
ISBN 1-55532-920-9

North American edition first published in 1989 by

Gareth Stevens Children's Books
7317 West Green Tree Road
Milwaukee, Wisconsin 53223, USA

Series editor: Valerie Weber
Research editor: Scott Enk
Cover design: Laurie Shock

1 2 3 4 5 6 7 8 9 94 93 92 91 90 89

YOUNG EXPLORERS

ARCTIC EXPEDITION

Written by Mike Salisbury
Illustrated by Paul Johnson

CONTENTS

Arctic Circle Profile 4
Early Explorers 6
Arctic Equipment 8
Travel and Survival 10
Large Tundra Animals 12
Small Tundra Animals 14
Arctic Birds 16
Sea Birds 18
Ocean Life 20
Polar Bears 22
Arctic People 24
Arctic Update 28
For More Information 30
Index 32

Gareth Stevens Children's Books • Milwaukee

ARCTIC CIRCLE PROFILE

The Arctic is a region of land and sea surrounding the North Pole, the northernmost point on Earth. The Arctic Circle is an imaginary line around the North Pole at a latitude of 66°30' north. In the center of the Arctic Circle is the Arctic Ocean, partly covered by a huge sheet of floating ice.

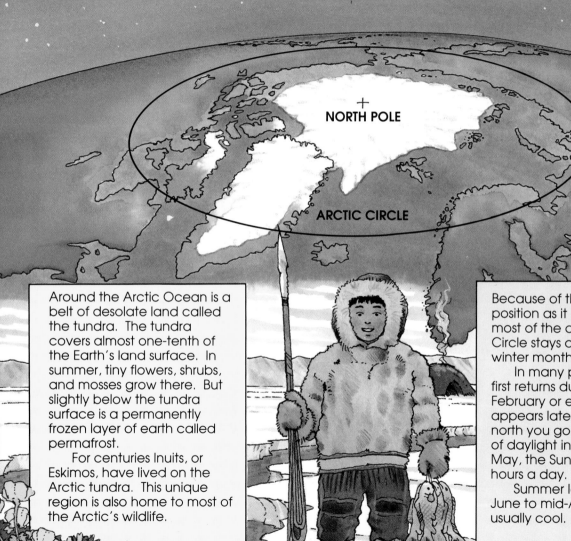

+ NORTH POLE

ARCTIC CIRCLE

Around the Arctic Ocean is a belt of desolate land called the tundra. The tundra covers almost one-tenth of the Earth's land surface. In summer, tiny flowers, shrubs, and mosses grow there. But slightly below the tundra surface is a permanently frozen layer of earth called permafrost.

For centuries Inuits, or Eskimos, have lived on the Arctic tundra. This unique region is also home to most of the Arctic's wildlife.

Because of the Earth's position as it orbits the Sun, most of the area in the Arctic Circle stays dark during the winter months.

In many places, the Sun first returns during late February or early March. It appears later the farther north you go. Then the hours of daylight increase, until by May, the Sun shines for 24 hours a day.

Summer lasts from mid-June to mid-August, but it is usually cool.

Around the edge of the tundra is a tree line, where the Earth's northern forests end. Beyond this line, the average temperature goes no higher than 50°F (10°C) even in the summer so most trees don't survive. Because of this, the tree line might be called the true boundary of the Arctic region.

In winter, the tundra is cold and icy. Fierce winds blow the snow into drifts, exposing various patches of land.

In summer, the top layer of tundra ground thaws. But the melted snow cannot drain through the permafrost, and much of the tundra becomes dotted with shallow lakes and ponds.

Arctic plants have only two months to reproduce, but when they do bloom, the tundra is transformed into a colorful garden.

The plants grow close to the ground to protect themselves from the cold and wind. The temperature in this low-lying carpet of foliage can be up to 68°F (20°C) warmer than the surrounding air. On dry land, you might see dwarf buttercups, shrubs, heathers, and poppies. Some plants have hairy leaves and stems that keep them warm. The few trees and shrubs that can exist in this harsh climate are stunted.

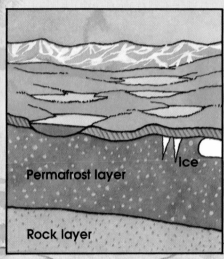

Permafrost layer

Ice

Rock layer

EARLY EXPLORERS

Many areas in the Arctic are named after early explorers, who had many dangerous and amazing adventures.

The first European to reach the Arctic may have been the Greek explorer Pytheas in about 325 B.C. He may have reached Iceland. But on his return, his fellow Greeks did not believe him. Then, some Irish monks rediscovered Iceland in the ninth century A.D. Bands of Vikings soon arrived and settled farther north in Greenland, where they met with the Inuit.

A Viking longboat

Henry Hudson cast adrift

In 1845, two British Navy ships under the command of Sir John Franklin disappeared while searching for the legendary Northwest Passage. Some say they did find the passage opening, but search parties found no sign of the ships.

Franklin's widow financed a final search that revealed that Franklin had died in 1847 and that the crew had abandoned the ship. But to this day, the bodies of Sir John Franklin and most of his crew have not been found.

It was not until 1906 that Norwegian explorer Roald Amundsen, with a six-member crew and a tiny ship called the *Gjøa*, finally found a way through the Arctic Ocean to the Pacific Ocean.

Between 1500 and 1900, many other explorers tried to find the Northwest Passage, the sea route from Europe to China via the Arctic Ocean. When the sixteenth-century Englishman Sir Martin Frobisher reached the Arctic, he was convinced that he had found the passage — and gold! Frobisher Bay on Canada's Baffin Island is named after him.

In 1610, the Englishman Henry Hudson sailed into the Arctic bay now named after him. He thought he too had found the passage and, despite storms and pack ice, wanted to continue. But his crew mutinied and cast him adrift with his son and a few men.

The search for Franklin

Ross meets an Inuit

In 1829, Sir John Ross and his nephew James Clark Ross set out to find the Northwest Passage, but their ship became stuck in the ice for three winters. During this time, they befriended the Inuit people who helped them to survive. James Clark Ross also mapped many Arctic islands and found the north magnetic pole, the only place in the world a compass points to, a different point than the true North Pole.

Eventually the ice crushed the Rosses' ship, but after many difficulties and adventures, the crew members were finally rescued.

Many Arctic explorers have tried to reach the North Pole. In 1893, Norwegian scientist Fridtjof Nansen started for the Arctic Ocean. That September, the sea froze around his ship, the *Fram*. But because of its carefully designed round hull, the ship rose onto the ice surface instead of being crushed.

The *Fram* drifted slowly nearer to the North Pole with the ice. Then Nansen and a companion set out to reach the Pole on foot. They eventually got to within 200 miles (322 km) of their goal — nearer than any previous explorer had gotten. On their return journey, they nearly starved, but they were finally rescued in June 1896.

The *Fram*

The *Nautilus*

There are several theories about who first reached the North Pole. Traditionally, the United States explorer Robert Peary, his assistant Matthew Henson, and their Inuit guides are credited with arriving at this goal.

In 1959, the U.S. Navy's atomic submarine *Nautilus* pioneered a new type of Arctic travel when it became the first submarine to cross the Arctic underneath the ice.

Now you can fly to the Arctic, land near the North Pole, and be back in a northern weather station, all within 24 hours — but that's not really exploring!

ARCTIC EQUIPMENT

If you go on an Arctic expedition, it's important that you take the right equipment. Some of the items you will need are shown below.

You must be sure to take the right clothing because it has to keep you warm enough to survive! You could either get a set of Inuit clothes made from animal skin (see p. 25) or take with you the clothes shown below. Either way, you should wear as many layers as you can because layers help create warm air pockets around your body.

Bright Arctic sunlight reflects strongly off the white snow and ice. This can lead to snow blindness, a painful condition that makes your eyes feel as if they are full of sharp dust! High-quality dark glasses will filter out the harmful light rays.

INSIDE LAYERS   OUTER LAYERS

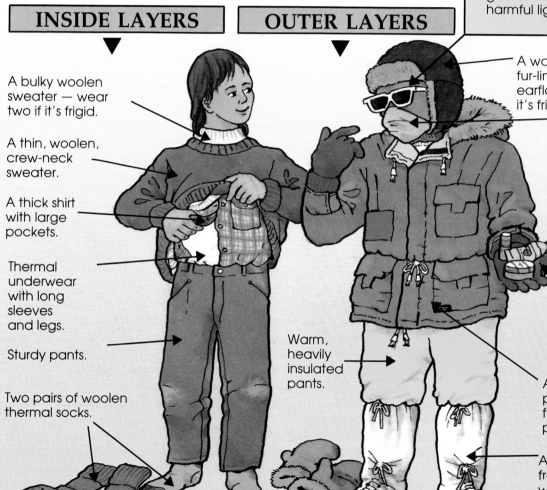

A bulky woolen sweater — wear two if it's frigid.

A thin, woolen, crew-neck sweater.

A thick shirt with large pockets.

Thermal underwear with long sleeves and legs.

Sturdy pants.

Two pairs of woolen thermal socks.

Warm, heavily insulated pants.

A warm hat, woolen or fur-lined. Hats with earflaps are good if it's frigid.

A face mask for snowmobile travel in temperatures below about 5°F (-15°C). This will help prevent frostbite on your nose cheeks, and mouth.

Sunscreen cream and lip salve. In summer on the tundra, you will also need insect repellant — there are mosquitoes by the millions!

A tough, windproof, padded jacket with a fur-lined hood and a pair of mitts.

Arctic boots made from thick white nylon with several layers of insulating material on the inside.

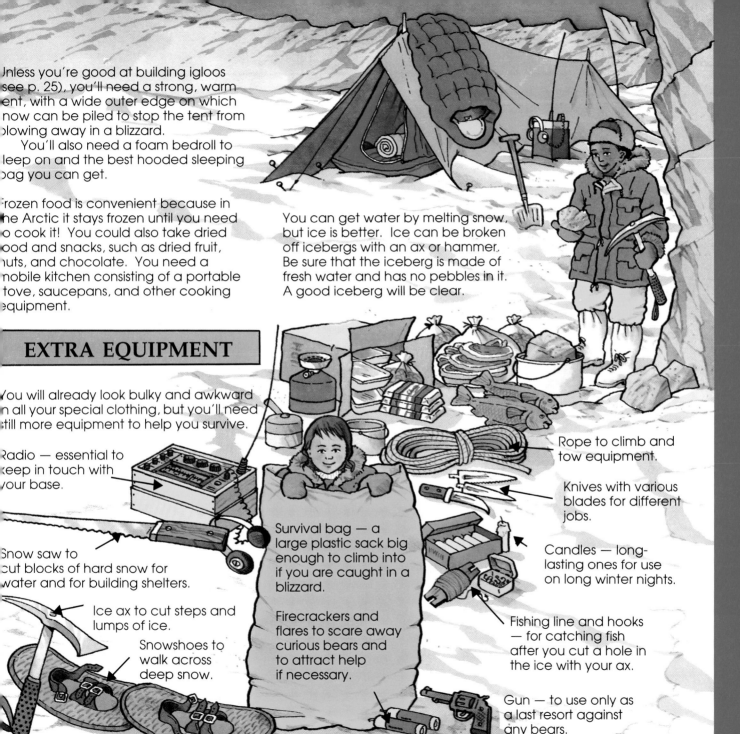

Unless you're good at building igloos (see p. 25), you'll need a strong, warm tent, with a wide outer edge on which snow can be piled to stop the tent from blowing away in a blizzard.

You'll also need a foam bedroll to sleep on and the best hooded sleeping bag you can get.

Frozen food is convenient because in the Arctic it stays frozen until you need to cook it! You could also take dried food and snacks, such as dried fruit, nuts, and chocolate. You need a mobile kitchen consisting of a portable stove, saucepans, and other cooking equipment.

You can get water by melting snow, but ice is better. Ice can be broken off icebergs with an ax or hammer. Be sure that the iceberg is made of fresh water and has no pebbles in it. A good iceberg will be clear.

EXTRA EQUIPMENT

You will already look bulky and awkward in all your special clothing, but you'll need still more equipment to help you survive.

Radio — essential to keep in touch with your base.

Snow saw to cut blocks of hard snow for water and for building shelters.

Ice ax to cut steps and lumps of ice.

Snowshoes to walk across deep snow.

Survival bag — a large plastic sack big enough to climb into if you are caught in a blizzard.

Firecrackers and flares to scare away curious bears and to attract help if necessary.

Rope to climb and tow equipment.

Knives with various blades for different jobs.

Candles — long-lasting ones for use on long winter nights.

Fishing line and hooks — for catching fish after you cut a hole in the ice with your ax.

Gun — to use only as a last resort against any bears.

9

TRAVEL AND SURVIVAL

Arctic travel is difficult and dangerous. If you don't plan carefully, your trip could end in disaster!

Husky dog teams and wooden sleds used to be the only method of Arctic winter travel.

Now, Arctic travelers use snowmobiles. They are similar to motorbikes but have skis at the front and a ribbed belt at the back.

Walking was once the only way to cross the land in summer, but now you can use an A.T.V. (All-Terrain Vehicle), a motorized tricycle with three balloon tires. These help absorb bumps and keep the A.T.V. from sinking in boggy ground.

To get to the farthest reaches of the Arctic, it is best to travel by airplane or helicopter. The most popular aircraft is probably the De Havilland Twin Otter. It can land or take off in distances as

short as 656 feet (200 m) and can be fitted with skis or balloon tires.

Helicopters can land on small patches of ground or even on drifting ice floes. However, they use a lot of fuel, so for long journeys you would need to organize fuel stations along your expedition route.

Journeys over Arctic pack ice can be dangerous because storms or tides can cause large areas of sea ice to break up and start moving. If you see cracks widening, hurry to a firmer area immediately!

A change of wind or tide can bring ice floes together, crushing all but the strongest ships. Only icebreaker ships with reinforced hulls can make any headway through the ice.

A.T.V.

Snowmobile

Expedition difficulties are often due to isolation from human help. The average distance from the tree line to the North Pole is 1,430 miles (2,300 km), and in all that distance, you might meet only a few people!

Radio contact is crucial. In the Canadian Arctic, explorers must report to a base station twice each day, at 7 a.m. and at 7 p.m.

If you miss three of your radio calls, a rescue plane will be sent to look for you. But if you simply forgot to call in, you will have to pay for the cost of the search!

Inuit families have their own radio frequencies for contacting each other. It is difficult to have a private radio conversation since there are often many other people listening in on each radio frequency!

Blowing snow sometimes causes whiteouts that can start without warning and last for days. In these conditions, it is impossible to see anything.

If you get caught in a difficult place, such as on a glacier, stop and camp until the whiteout is over. To be prepared in an emergency, always carry your tent, sleeping bag, and rations with you.

Arctic survival depends on keeping warm. The greatest danger is wind chill — when a strong wind brings the cooling effect of cold air down to dangerous levels. In cold weather, even a mild wind can cause bare flesh to freeze within one minute. So if the wind gets fierce, find shelter immediately— dig a hole in the snow if necessary!

Two major dangers in the Arctic are frostbite and hypothermia. The first signs of hypothermia are shivering and drowsiness. It should be quickly stopped with hot drinks and a warm sleeping bag. Frostbite starts on the hands, feet, and face. First the skin goes white and then all feeling is lost. The best cure is to gently warm the area. For frostbitten feet, for example, put your feet on someone's stomach.

LARGE TUNDRA ANIMALS

Most Arctic animals live on the tundra only during the summer months, finding shelter in the forests or underground during winter. Some of the largest tundra creatures are shown below.

Grizzly bears sleep in dens during winter, so you would probably only see one between March and late October.

Grizzlies eat grass, berries, insects, small mammals, fish, and sometimes caribou. They might even visit your camp if they can smell your food!

A grizzly may give you little warning of an attack. If one comes your way, back slowly and calmly away. With luck, the bear will then lose interest.

The most common large Arctic animal is the tundra deer. It is usually called a caribou in North America and a reindeer in Europe.

In Scandinavia, the Lapp people keep reindeer in herds. In Canada and Alaska, the caribou roam freely, gathering into vast herds to travel from the winter home in the forests to the summer home on the tundra. A moving herd is an amazing wildlife spectacle — sometimes thousands of animals roam together across the tundra.

Grizzly bear

Wolverine

The wolverine is one of the rarest animals in the tundra, seen only in remote areas. An adult can grow up to about 39 inches (1 m) long.

To keep warm, wolverines have two sets of fur — a thick, soft inner fur with larger hairs forming an outer layer.

Wolverines are solitary creatures. They range over large territories, which they mark out with a distinctive musky odor. They eat small mammals, baby caribou, and dead and decaying animals. They also eat berries when they can find them.

Musk oxen defend their herd

Musk ox herds are peaceful, but if a predator such as a wolf or a bear appears, the adults form a defensive ring facing outward and one of the bulls will charge to scare off the enemy. From mid-July through September, the oxen mate and the strongest male tries to chase off his rivals. The oxen charge at each other and sometimes crash head-on at speeds up to 31 miles (50 km) an hour!

Musk oxen graze on the tundra all year long. They have large curved horns and are covered in an outer coat of dense, long hair. Beneath this coat is a layer of fine wool that they shed each spring when the weather gets warmer. Small birds often gather the discarded fleece from rocks and bushes to make cozy nests.

Arctic wolf

Wolves can often be seen following caribou herds. Wolf fur ranges in color from almost black to pure white. They live in packs, hunting together by chasing their prey into an ambush or running in relays to keep a herd in turmoil until a weak animal can be picked off.

Sometimes wolves howl together in an eerie chorus that biologists think may help to keep a pack together. You can hear the noise up to 10 miles (16 km) away. People have feared and hunted wolves for centuries, but in reality, wolf attacks on humans are rare.

SMALL TUNDRA ANIMALS

There are many small animals on the tundra throughout the year. Some of them stay above the snow surface in winter, and some hide in burrows under the hard crust of snow.

Ermine

Several species of lemmings also live in underground burrows during winter. These small rodents feed on grass and buried plant roots.

The lemmings begin to breed in spring and their numbers increase quickly, causing regular population explosions every four years or so. Then some migrate to new feeding areas to avoid famine. Many die of exhaustion and starvation on the journey or drown trying to swim across water. The number of lemmings is reduced this way and the four-year cycle starts again.

Arctic ground squirrels build elaborate tunnel systems underground. Many different species of animals use these tunnels to hibernate from November to March.

Many animals rely on lemmings for food. For example, weasels and ermines are small enough to chase lemmings down their burrows and eat them.

In winter, ermine fur turns white. It is highly prized by human hunters.

Ground squirrel

Weasel

Collared lemmings

The white Arctic hares are the largest hares in the world. They can weigh up to 12 pounds (5.5 kg). When the icy wind blows strongly, they will sit for hours with their ears back and their legs tucked under their bodies. Sometimes they will dig tunnels in the snow for shelter.

Arctic fox

Arctic hare

In winter, Arctic foxes are pure white or even blue, but in the summer their fur turns a smoky gray. In some areas, they feed mainly on lemmings and adjust the number of cubs that are born each spring according to the lemming population — the more lemmings there are, the larger the fox litter.

Foxes are always searching for food and will eat eggs, birds, berries, and small animals. Sometimes they follow polar bears far out onto the sea ice to feed on leftover scraps of food. They will often appear at camps looking for scraps. Foxes have a keen intelligence and little fear of humans. Hunters trap and kill many thousands for their fur every year.

Arctic lemming

Brown lemming

Arctic hares mate in April and May after boxing matches and extraordinary running and leaping displays by the males.

Some Arctic hares herd together in one place in groups of hundreds, or even thousands. They feed and run in a tightly bunched mass that can be easily mistaken for a patch of mysteriously flowing snow!

ARCTIC BIRDS

Over 100 different species of bird breed in the Arctic, but most of these are summer visitors. Few species are adapted to survive the extreme cold, the darkness, and the lack of food in winter.

WINTER BIRDS

Ptarmigan have speckled brown plumage in summer and white plumage in winter. It even grows on their legs and feet. In frigid weather, they sometimes burrow under the snow to look for warmth and willow shoots or old berries.

Snowy owl

Ptarmigan

The brilliant white snowy owl makes an unforgettable sight as it stares with piercing eyes or swoops silently down to snatch its prey.
  The owl survives the winter by eating any animals it finds — including any hares, mice, or lemmings foolish enough to come to the snow surface.

During winter, you may hear a raven's croak. Ravens and Arctic redpolls winter near the tundra tree line.

Raven

Redpoll

SUMMER BIRDS

The Arctic summer lasts for barely two months, so birds visiting from the south must arrive as soon as the snow begins to clear in late May. They raise their young as quickly as possible and fly south again before the end of August, when harsh winter weather begins to return to the tundra.

Many geese return in May, flying in spectacular V-shaped formations. Common kinds include the brent, white-fronted, pink-footed, barnacle, and greater and lesser snow geese.
  To avoid any predators, especially Arctic foxes, which don't like to swim, geese often nest on small islands or take their goslings to tundra lakes as soon as they possibly can.

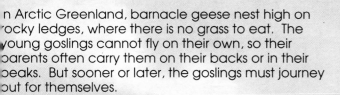

In Arctic Greenland, barnacle geese nest high on rocky ledges, where there is no grass to eat. The young goslings cannot fly on their own, so their parents often carry them on their backs or in their beaks. But sooner or later, the goslings must journey out for themselves.

In summer, over 30 types of waders and several diving birds come to feed in the tundra lakes and ponds. One example is the red-throated diver bird, which can stay under water for up to three minutes.

Widgeon

Teal

Old squaw

Phalarope

Plover

Turnstone

Eider duck

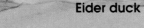

Many species of ducks nest near the tundra lakes where they feed. Examples include the widgeon, the teal, and the pintail.

Around deeper lakes you may see diving ducks such as the merganser, the old squaw, and the common and king eider ducks.

Arctic birds of prey include buzzards, peregrines, and gyrfalcons, which catch small birds in midair after frightening them into leaving their nests.

Many small migrant birds, such as larks, wheatears, and pipits, come to feed on the summer supply of insects. Snow buntings are the first to arrive each April and their songs bring the tundra alive after the long winter.

Gyrfalcon

Snow bunting

SEA BIRDS

Millions of sea birds migrate northward each summer to breed in the Arctic. They take advantage of the plentiful food supply that is uncovered when the ice breaks up. Some common species are shown below.

Fulmars are graceful, gliding flyers with narrow wings. They catch small fish and crustaceans in the open patches of water between ice floes.

The fulmars mate each year around late April or early May. Their traditional nesting sites become crowded and noisy, with sometimes up to 100,000 breeding pairs in one area.

When a particularly popular fulmar breeding area is shared by two other major kinds of cliff-nesting birds, the guillemot and the kittiwake, the sight is spectacular.

On the world-famous cliffs of Prince Leopold Island in the Canadian Arctic, more than half a million sea bird pairs nest in summer. This amazing sight has deservedly been called one of the bird-watching wonders of the world.

Fulmar

Kittiwake

Guillemot

Little auk

Glaucous gull

Ivory gull

Little auks are the most abundant of all the sea birds that breed in the Arctic. They nest on rocky slopes in gigantic colonies. The total number of pairs visiting the Arctic each summer has been estimated to be 17.5 million — that's 35 million individual birds!

Large gray glaucous gulls breed on the Arctic cliffs in smaller numbers. They prey on the other birds, patrolling nesting ledges looking for unattended eggs or chicks to eat.

Of all the gulls you might see in the north, the most truly Arctic is the ivory gull, a beautiful creamy white bird with yellow legs and a pale yellow bill.
    These gulls breed in small groups on isolated rocky shorelines, feeding mostly amid the pack ice. In winter they move only as far as the southern edge of the Arctic ice.

Arctic terns nest on shoreline tundra or shingle banks. They catch fish and plankton to feed to their nestlings. These chicks develop quickly during July and August in readiness for the longest of all bird migrations known to scientists.
    The terns leave the Arctic each fall. Their long journey takes them down the entire length of the Atlantic and Pacific oceans and on to the Antarctic pack ice at the other end of the world. They make the return journey the following June. This breathtaking trek is an amazing feat of endurance for such a small bird.

OCEAN LIFE

Arctic sea temperatures range from approximately -40°F (-40°C) in winter to just above freezing by the end of summer. The cold water would quickly kill unprotected humans, but Arctic animals such as seals, walrus, and whales have warm layers of insulating fat called blubber for protection.

Although the surface of the sea ice may be frozen and lifeless, the underside is quite different. From March through August, sunlight filters through almost 6.5 feet (2 m) of ice, and a layer of greenish brown algae grows on the ice undersurface. These simple plants form the basis of the food chain on which all Arctic sea creatures depend.

Many tiny shrimplike creatures called amphipods graze upside-down on the algae. The amphipods, in turn, are eaten by polar and Arctic cod. Both cod and amphipods are eaten by whales, seals, and sea birds. At the top of the food chain is the polar bear, which feeds mainly on seals.

Ringed seal

Ringed seals stay in the Arctic all year round, living mostly under the ice and basking on the surface in summer. To survive under the ice, seals must keep a breathing hole open. Using their teeth and flippers, they dig out a funnel-shaped hole to the surface with an opening to the air. In spring, a pregnant ringed seal will make a birth lair, a chamber next to a breathing hole, where it will give birth to one pup. The lair helps to hide the family from hungry polar bears.

Bearded seals also live in the Arctic all year round and keep breathing holes open in winter. Their name comes from their beard of stiff sensitive hairs that they use to feel along the sea-bed for food.
Bearded seal hide is strong and waterproof. Inuits prize the hide and use it for making boots and skin-covered boats.

Bearded seal

Walrus are famous for their ivory tusks, which can extend over 3 feet (1 m) long on an adult male. These hefty creatures can weigh up to 3,000 pounds (1,360 kg), but this bulk does not affect their swimming. They become fast and graceful in the water.

Once the walrus reach the bottom, they find shellfish and crush them between their teeth. Then they suck out the food from inside. They sometimes kill and eat seals, so if you are near them, be careful — they might mistake you for a seal!

Walrus

Harp seals

Harp seals spend the frigid Arctic winter south of the pack ice and swim north in the spring, grouping together in huge numbers to breed.

The pups are born toward the end of each February. For the first 4 weeks or so, the seal pups have pure white fur. Canadian hunters once killed thousands of pups every year but worldwide publicity about the cruelty of the hunt forced the hunters to reduce or stop the killing.

Three species of whales live amid the Arctic pack ice. One of these is named the right whale. Because it was slow and easy to catch, whalers considered it the "right" creature to hunt.

Right whales have a curved upper jaw hung with a curtain of fiberlike plates. As the right whale swims, water is forced through the plates, which act like giant sieves and trap amphipods for the whale to eat.

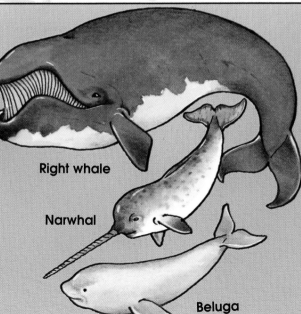

Right whale

Narwhal

Beluga

The other two truly Arctic whales are the beluga, or white whale, and the narwhal. Both species gather to feed on amphipods and fish at the floe edge — the place where the Arctic ice sheet meets the ocean.

Narwhals are sometimes known as sea unicorns, because the males grow an extraordinary spiraled tusk, sometimes 9 feet (3 m) long.

Adult belugas are pure white and show up beautifully in the clear Arctic waters.

POLAR BEARS

Nanuk is the Inuit name for the polar bear. It is the most impressive, most feared animal found roaming the Arctic, and no visit would be complete without seeing one.

Adult male polar bears can weigh more than 1,550 pounds (600 kg) and measure 11 feet (3.3 m) from nose to tail. This makes the polar bear one of the largest land carnivores in the world.

The polar bear has large teeth designed for tearing prey and claws as sharp as a tiger's.

Polar bears have a sensitive nose. As a bear wanders across the ice, it will frequently point its head upward to sniff the air, testing for the faintest smell that might lead to a seal — or a tent where explorers are cooking their breakfast. Polar bears have been known to detect prey from several miles away.

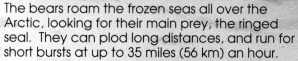

The bears roam the frozen seas all over the Arctic, looking for their main prey, the ringed seal. They can plod long distances, and run for short bursts at up to 35 miles (56 km) an hour.

Considering their great size, polar bears are remarkably agile, and they can swim well, diving to depths of several yards for up to two minutes.

One of the ways they catch seals unawares is to glide slowly toward one, with only their head above water. However, most seals are caught by bears crouching patiently for hours by a breathing hole, waiting to catch the seal when it emerges.

Mating occurs in spring. Then, when winter comes, the pregnant females wander into the coastal hills and valleys to find places where there are snowdrifts. Here they dig their maternity den so that by midwinter, when they give birth to between 1 and 3 cubs, they will be totally hidden under the surface.

In early summer, the female bears break out of their den. They often slide down the slopes and roll on their backs in what looks like sheer delight at being back outside. Since they have not eaten since about November, they emerge thin and hungry. Within a few days, a mother bear will take her cubs on short outings to strengthen their legs.

Mothers are attentive to their cubs, stopping to rest and suckle them frequently. But these first weeks are extremely dangerous and many cubs die. The cubs can get lost and separated from their mother, and killer whales, walrus, and unthinking humans can also pose a great risk to the cubs.

Cubs that do survive stay with their mother for at least a year, learning from her and practicing various ways to catch seals until they can manage on their own.

Polar bears will feast on berries and other vegetation in season, but they are also fascinated by anything they think might be tasty, including expedition equipment such as tents, boots, rubber boats, snowmobile seats, engine oil, and even humans!

The best way to scare a bear away is to use flares or firecrackers. If these don't work, your last resort is a gun. But it is much better to be on guard for bears and deter them before they get too close.

ARCTIC PEOPLE

The people of the Arctic were once called Eskimo, which means "eaters of raw flesh" in North American Indian language. This referred to their habit of eating uncooked meat. The name was probably originally meant as an insult, and the Arctic inhabitants now prefer to be called Inuit — which in their language means "the people."

There are about 100,000 Inuit living in Greenland, Alaska, Canada, and Siberia. They speak two main languages — Yupik in southwestern Alaska and Siberia, and Inupiaq from Alaska across Canada to Greenland. There are many different dialects within these two main language groups.

For at least 4,000 years, groups of Inuit have hunted animals for food and clothing. They developed a nomadic way of life, settling for short periods where the hunting was good, building igloo shelters, and then moving on when the animals were gone.

Some Inuit continue to follow this pattern while others have settled in one place.

Inuit knowledge has been passed on orally for centuries. The Inuit have a long tradition of storytelling — a good way of spending the long hours of winter darkness. Their favorite stories are funny and courageous tales of hunting exploits. Inuits used to build especially large igloos in winter so that groups could get together to listen to stories.

Traditional Inuit houses vary depending on the season or area. The best-known is the snow igloo, a dome shape built from snow blocks. Inside a snow igloo, the Inuit spread out sleeping rugs of caribou or polar bear fur and light a stone lamp, which uses oil for fuel and cotton grass as a wick. It emits heat as well as light.

Inuits still build small igloos occasionally for overnight hunting stops. Large snow igloos built as meeting places are more luxurious, with snow benches and windows made from ice sheets. Today, the Inuit use roomy canvas tents in summer, but they used to make traditional tents from walrus hides and driftwood poles.

Many Inuit now wear modern clothes, but their traditional dress is much warmer.

Caribou or bearskin jackets are made loose-fitting so that the wearer will not get hot and uncomfortable. The hood is usually trimmed with fur.

Big fur mitts, usually of wolf skin, keep the hands warm.

Traditional pants are made from animal skins. The warmest pairs have two layers, one with fur facing the inside and one with fur facing the outside.

The best Arctic boots are made of waterproof skins, sewn together with walrus-hide thread that swells up when wet and keeps water from seeping in through the needle holes. Sometimes these boots have an inner lining of soft fur or are stuffed with dry grass.

Many Inuit are artistic and often spend winter hours making traditional carvings from steatite (soapstone), ivory, wood, or bone.

ARCTIC PEOPLE — Continued

For centuries, everything the Inuit needed for food and clothing had to come from animals, so they developed great hunting skills, which some Inuit still use today. Even today, small children start to learn how to hunt at a young age.

Many Inuit find that their traditional hunting weapons are just as effective as modern rifles. The throwing spear, or harpoon, has always been their main weapon. At the end, it has a detachable toothed tip carved out of walrus or narwhal ivory. Attached to the harpoon is a long line that the hunter grabs to keep his prey from escaping.

During winter, seals must keep breathing holes open in the sea ice (see p. 20). Inuits use dogs to sniff out these spots. The hunter then sticks a thin piece of whalebone as a marker in the breathing hole.

Then the hunter crouches, sometimes without moving for many hours, waiting for the seal to return. As soon as the bone moves, the hunter thrusts downward with the harpoon and pulls the seal onto the surface of the ice.

Hunters stalk polar bears in late winter. A hunter will follow a set of bear tracks. When he spots his prey, he will let loose his fastest dogs to chase it. Quickly unloading luggage to lighten his sled, he then chases after the dogs. A bear will always head for open water and can escape by swimming away, but if the dogs corner the bear, the hunter can usually catch up and kill it.

In summer small canoes, called kayaks, are used for hunting belugas and narwhals (see p. 21). These craft are fast and maneuverable but they can be difficult to handle.

Whale meat is eaten raw and is a favorite traditional food. It is not only delicious but also provides a rich source of natural vitamins that would be destroyed by cooking.

Seals have good eyesight under water, but poor eyesight on land. Hunters can take advantage of this and creep up on a basking seal by mimicking a seal's bobbing movements. Another trick is to sneak up to a seal behind a white screen of skin with a tiny peephole in the middle. The screen blends with the surrounding snow so the seal does not see it.

← Inuksuit

Many Inuit groups traditionally move onto the tundra in the summer to hunt caribou. One traditional hunting method was to drive the animals into a valley or corral to be ambushed. Lines of person-sized piles of stones called *inuksuit*, meaning "like a person," were built along the ridges to scare the caribou and guide them toward the hunters, hidden in waiting.

To live by hunting requires an expert knowledge of animal behavior and a respect for nature. The Inuit wasted nothing — they used every animal part, skins, bones, and fat included.

Now, even with supplies of manufactured clothing and food, many Inuit hunt to provide for their families.

ARCTIC UPDATE

The Arctic is the largest wilderness area left in the world, and the skills of Inuit hunters have enabled them to live there for centuries without endangering its wildlife. But modern developments now increasingly threaten the Arctic environment.

The Arctic has rich reserves of oil and gas, but getting them out is expensive. The pipelines must be laid above ground, where they sometimes block the migrating routes of the caribou (see p. 12). One answer to this problem is to raise the pipelines into bridges.

(see p. 12)

The Arctic is rich in minerals, but moving heavy mining equipment across the tundra leaves deep tracks in the ground. Because Arctic plant growth is so slow, these scars on the land can last for fifty or more years.

To avoid this, workers make ice roads on frozen land and water for hundreds of miles.

Scientists are trying to learn more about the Arctic environment so they can limit damage to plants and wildlife as the oil and gas industries move into the area. Chemical waste is already polluting some areas. New expeditions can help by testing air and water for signs of pollution.

The Inuit have the best knowledge of Arctic survival, but many people are worried that their age-old culture will gradually die out as their way of life changes.

Although some Inuit groups still live traditionally, many have now moved into permanent modern settlements. They often work in the oil or mining industries. But their jobs are insecure and their families often live in poverty, having forgotten the old hunting skills.

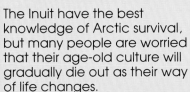

CONSERVING THE ARCTIC

With modern equipment and transportation, it's easier to get to the Arctic and exploit its natural resources. To prevent the bad effects of industrial pollution and other environmental dangers, we must explore the Arctic and learn about its fragile ecology. We must work to protect its unique wildlife and exciting landscape.

Some countries have already declared certain rich wildlife areas as reserves. International agreements have also limited hunting of endangered animals.

If you go to the Arctic one day, you might help to explore and preserve this amazing place!

FOR MORE INFORMATION

Magazines

Here are some children's magazines that may have articles about the Arctic and other polar regions. If your library or bookstore does not have them, write to the publishers listed below for information about subscribing.

Dodo Dispatch
34th Street and Girard
Philadelphia, PA 19104

Elsa's Echo
3201 Tepusquet Canyon
Santa Maria, CA 93454

National Geographic World
National Geographic Society
17th and M Streets NW
Washington, DC 20036

Ranger Rick
National Wildlife Federation
1412 16th Street NW
Washington, DC 20036

Owl
The Young Naturalist Foundation
59 Front Street East
Toronto, Ontario
Canada M5E 1B3

Tracks
P.O. Box 30235
Lansing, MI 48909

Addresses

The organizations listed below have information about the Arctic and the plant and animal species living there. When you write to them, tell them exactly what you want to know.

Division of Polar Programs
Polar Coordination and Information Section
Directorate for Geosciences
1800 G Street NW, Room 627
Washington, DC 20550

Arctic Biological Station
555 St. Pierre Boulevard
Ste. Anne de Belleview
Quebec H9X 3R4, Canada

Books

The following books concern polar regions and the people, plants, and animals that live there. If you are not able to find them in your library or bookstore, ask someone to order them for you.

Animals of the Polar Regions. Johnson (Lerner)
The Arctic. Hargreaves (Silver Burdett)
The Arctic and Antarctic. Sandak (Franklin Watts)
Arctic and Antarctic Regions. Sabin (Troll)
An Eskimo Family. Alexander and Alexander (Lerner)

Eskimos. Purdy and Sandak (Franklin Watts)
The Frozen North. Cuisin (Silver Burdett)
The Polar Bear. Ahlstrom (Crestwood House)
Polar Bears. Moore (Garrard)
The Seal on the Rocks. Allan (Oxford Scientific Films/Gareth Stevens)

Glossary

Baleen
The fibrous plates that hang in rows from the roof of the mouth of a whalebone whale. The whale uses these plates for straining food such as small fish, krill, and other forms of *plankton* from the water. One of the main reasons whaling became such a big industry in the nineteenth century was that baleen was especially strong and elastic. It was unlike most other materials then available. People used it in machinery, corsets, whips, umbrellas, and the peaks of caps. Plastic has now replaced it for many uses, and we no longer need to hunt the whales.

Magnetic North
The direction to which a compass points. True north is the direction toward the North Pole, the north end of the Earth's axis. The angle formed between true north and the magnetic north is called the magnetic declination. This angle varies from year to year and from place to place.

Nestling
A young bird while it is still in the nest. Usually young birds are hatched blind, naked, and helpless. The baby birds stay in the nest for some time and are completely dependent on their parents until they leave the nest.

Pack ice
A large area of floating ice formed on the sea where the seawater has frozen. The wind and sea currents drive pieces of floating ice together to make pack ice.

Permafrost
Ground that is permanently frozen. Large areas of permafrost cover parts of Canada, Alaska, northern Europe and Asia, and Antarctica. Greenland is almost completely covered in permafrost. It is difficult for people to build in the Arctic because the permafrost is so hard.

Plankton
Tiny plant and animal organisms that live in fresh or salt water. Most of the plants are algae, and most of the animals are tiny, one-celled creatures. The polar seas are particularly rich in plankton. Birds, seals, and blue and fin whales eat one kind of plankton, called krill. Plankton may also become an important food source for humans in the future.

Preserve
An area of land set aside and maintained for the protection of wildlife or natural resources.

Shingle
Beach gravel made up of large, smooth pebbles unmixed with finer materials such as sand.

Tundra
The treeless area between the ice cap and the tree line. *Permafrost* covers the ground. The northern tundra is sometimes called the desert of the north. Plants growing there must have short roots because the ground is frozen solid much of the year. They must also be suited to shallow, waterlogged soil, short summers, and cold winds.

Whiteout
A weather condition caused by heavy cloud cover over the snow. During a whiteout, the amount of light coming from the Sun above is almost equal to the amount of light reflected from the snow and ice on the ground. There are no shadows during a whiteout. The horizon is invisible and you can only see very dark objects.

Index

airplane 10
amphipods 20, 21
Amundsen, Roald 6
animals 12-24, 28, 29
    endangered 29
animal skin 8, 25
Arctic
    Canadian 11, 18
    Circle 4
    Ocean 4, 6
A.T.V. 10

bears
    grizzly 12
    polar 20, 22-23, 26
blubber 20
breathing hole 20, 22, 26

caribou 12, 27, 28
carvings 25
climate 4, 5, 11
clothes 8, 25, 27
conservation 29

De Havilland Twin Otter 10
ducks 17

equipment 8-9, 28, 29
ermine 14
Eskimo 4, 24
expeditions 6-7, 10-11, 28
explorers 6-7, 11, 22

firecrackers 9, 23
fish 9, 12, 18, 20
flares 9, 23
food 9, 24, 26, 27
fox, Arctic 15, 16
Franklin, Sir John 6
Frobisher, Sir Martin 6
frostbite 8, 11

geese 16-17
Gjøa 6

Greenland 6, 17, 24
ground squirrels 14

hare, white Arctic 15, 16
helicopter 10
hibernation 14
hunters 15, 21, 26
hunting 24, 26-27, 29
husky dogs 10
hypothermia 11

ice ax 9
icebergs 9
igloos 9, 24, 25
industry 28, 29
Inuit 4, 6, 7, 11, 20, 24-27, 29
inuksuit 27
Inupiaq 24

kayak 27

language 24
Lapps 12
lemmings 14, 15

musk oxen 13

Nansen, Fridtjof 7
nanuk 22
Nautilus 7
North Pole 4, 7, 11
Northwest Passage 6, 7

pack ice 6, 10, 19, 21
Peary, Robert 7
permafrost 4, 5
plankton 19
plants 5, 20, 28
polar bears 20, 22-23, 26
pollution 28, 29
Pytheas 6

radio 9, 11
reindeer 12

rodents 14-15
Ross, James Clarke 7
Ross, Sir John 7

sea birds 18-19
seals 20-21, 22, 26-27
shellfish 21
sleds 10, 26
snowmobiles 8, 10
snow saw 9
snowshoes 9
snowy owl 16
submarine 7
summer 4, 5, 8, 10
survival bag 9

temperature 4, 5, 20
tent 9, 11, 25
tides 10
travel 10-11
tree line 5
trees 5
tundra 4, 5, 16, 17, 27

walrus 21
weasels 14
whales 20, 21, 27
whiteouts 11
wind chill 11
winter 4, 5
wolverine 12
wolves 13

Yupik 24

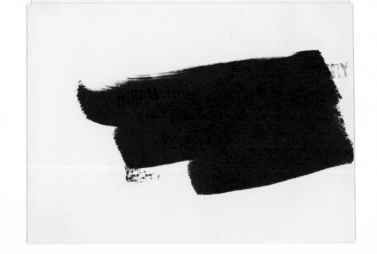